WALKS ARO SKIPTON

10 WALKS EACH 6 MILES OR LESS

Dalesman

First published in 2006 by Dalesman
an imprint of
Country Publications Ltd
The Water Mill
Broughton Hall
Skipton
North Yorkshire BD23 3AG

Reprinted 2008

Text © Mark Reid 2006
Maps © Gelder Design & Mapping 2006
Illustrations © Christine Isherwood 2006

Cover: Crookrise Crag by Colin Raw

A British Library Cataloguing-in-Publication record
is available for this book

ISBN 978-1-85568-219-1

Printed by Amadeus Press, Cleckheaton

PUBLISHER'S NOTE
The information given in this book has been provided in good faith and is intended only
as a general guide. Whilst all reasonable efforts have been made to ensure that details
were correct at the time of publication, the author and Country Publications Ltd
cannot accept any responsibility for inaccuracies. It is the responsibility of individuals
undertaking outdoor activities to approach the activity with caution and, especially if
inexperienced, to do so under appropriate supervision. The activity described in this book
is strenuous and individuals should ensure that they are suitably fit before embarking
upon it. They should carry the appropriate equipment and maps, be properly clothed and
have adequate footwear. They should also take note of weather conditions and forecasts,
and leave notice of their intended route and estimated time of return.

Contents

Introduction

Skipton is often described as the 'Gateway to the Yorkshire Dales', a title which actually means that most people drive through the town *en route* to Malham, Grassington, the Three Peaks or the Lake District. In fact, for many years this is exactly what I did, although I always wondered what it would be like to climb Sharp Haw or Embsay Crag. Now I know.

Skipton lies at the heart of Airedale, where gritstone meets limestone, where the farming landscape of the Yorkshire Dales meets the old mill villages of the South Pennines. Here is a landscape full of interest and history, with monastic remains, a steam-hauled railway, England's longest inland waterway, a mighty castle, attractive villages and some great pubs, rolling heather moorland, gritstone crags and superb viewpoints. All of the right ingredients for some great walking.

The highlight for me was the walk from Lothersdale up to Pinhaw on Carleton Moor. It was a cold, crisp January day, and the air was sharp and bright. A steady climb across pastures and then heather moorland brought me to the trig point on Pinhaw and a 'wow!' moment. Sitting down resting against the OS column, I soaked up one of the finest views I had seen, with the hills and mountains of the southern Yorkshire Dales laid out before me. I followed the skyline sweeping east to west, naming the peaks as I went: Simons Seat, Great Whernside, Buckden Pike, Penyghent, Ingleborough, Pendle Hill and the rugged peaks of Lakeland on the horizon.

Skipton is surrounded by hills and moors as well as valleys and farmland, which means that many of these walks take in a variety of terrain, including open heather moorland, riverside paths, woodland, boggy ground, countless 'squeeze-stiles', and some 'short but sharp' ascents and descents that will certainly bring some colour to your cheeks. Good walking boots and suitable waterproof clothing are essential at all times, as is a packed lunch and a drink to enjoy whilst taking in the scenery. Of course, only head out into the hills if you have an Ordnance Survey map with you — OS Explorer Maps OL2 (Yorkshire Dales Southern & Western areas) and OL21 (South Pennines) cover these walks.

Bolton Bridge

Distance: 3 miles (5 km)
Time: 1¹/₂ hours
**Terrain: Field paths all the way. The descent through Lob Wood is
steep in places, with drops to the side of the path. This walk
crosses the A59 at Bolton Bridge at the start of the walk and also
includes a short section of road walking along the B6160 towards
the end.**
Start: parking area near 'old' Bolton Bridge, grid ref 071529

*Bolton Bridge is a delightful hamlet beside the River Wharfe at the very
southern edge of the Yorkshire Dales National Park. A new bridge now
carries the busy Skipton to Harrogate road, leaving the old seventeenth-
century bridge delightfully traffic-free.*

From the parking area near the old bridge, head right along the road, passing
the Devonshire Arms Hotel. Take the turning to the left just after the
Devonshire Club by the turning circle through a gate across the road (this
was the old Harrogate to Skipton road prior to the bypass). Head along this
road for a short distance. Take the path to the left down some steps, and bear
to the right across the field to reach a footbridge across Hambleton Beck.
After the footbridge, head straight on alongside the wall on your left. At the
gate in the field corner, turn right along an old grassy track up to reach a stile
at the top of the field that leads down to reach the A59.

Cross over the road (with care), and take the footpath opposite up some
steps and over a stile. Follow the clear path straight on, with woodland on
your right, to quickly reach a gate, after which head up along the grassy
track alongside the wall on your right to reach an old railway bridge across
the former Skipton to Ilkley branch line.

*This railway was built during the 1880s to create a direct route from Leeds
through to Skipton via Ilkley. However, it closed in 1965, although part of
the line has since reopened as the Embsay and Bolton Abbey Steam Railway.*

Head over the railway bridge and continue up along the grassy track,
keeping close to the wall on your right, then, where the wall bends away to

the right, carry straight on up to reach a gate in a wall at the top of the field. Head through the gate, then bear slightly to the left across the field to a stile across a fence. Head to the right, gradually slanting up across the flanks of Haw Pike, heading towards the whitewashed Berwick East Farm set in some trees. As you reach a wall across your path just before the farm buildings, turn left alongside this wall to quickly reach a wooden gate to the right of a house (Berwick Cottage) that leads onto a driveway. Turn right along the driveway and follow it, bending round to the left through a gate to join the access road from Berwick East Farm. Turn left along this road, then immediately head to the left alongside the wall on your left up through an area of young trees to reach a stile over a fence, after which head up to reach a wall-stile in the top left corner of the field.

Cross the stile and head straight on alongside the wall on your left to reach another wall-stile beside a gate in the field corner. Cross this stile, turn right (the wall now on your right) and follow the wall to reach three gates in the corner of the field. Head through the gate in the corner that leads out onto a field by the last of the four large wind turbines (Chelker Reservoir down to the right).

These huge wind turbines are impressive to say the least viewed at close quarters, their huge blades turning hypnotically with a great whirring sound. These turbines can produce 1.2 megawatts of electricity which, put another way, is enough to power about 750 homes.

Head straight on alongside the wall on your left, passing the wind turbine, then down to reach a gate in the corner of the field. Follow the wall bending round to the left to join a grassy track, which you continue on to reach a gate across your path in a 'dog-leg' in the wall beside two stone buildings. Head through the gate and take the grassy track diagonally across the field to join a wall on your right just beside a large pile of rubble set in some trees (formerly Hag Head Laithe barn).

Continue straight on along the track to reach a gate in the corner of the field. After the gate, head straight on alongside the wall on your right (do not continue along the track) to reach a wall-stile in the bottom corner of the field. After the wall-stile, bear to the right down across the hillside (heading towards Bolton Bridge in the valley bottom). Arrive at another wall-stile in the bottom corner of the field that leads into Lob Wood.

The views from this hillside are superb, with the rocky outcrops of Simons Seat rising above the remains of Bolton Priory, Bolton Bridge reposing in the valley beneath Beamsley Beacon and lower Wharfedale curving down towards Ilkley.

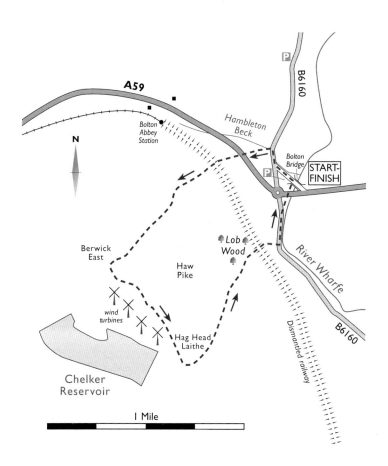

Cross the stile and follow the path to the right through woodland alongside the wall on your right. After about fifty yards, follow the path to the left dropping steeply down some steps into the wooded gorge of Lob Wood. After passing beneath the old railway viaduct, the path gradually drops down to reach the main road (B6160). Turn left along the road (take care) with the River Wharfe to your right. Just before you reach the roundabout, take the footpath to the right, marked by a signpost, over a footbridge across a side-stream. Follow the riverside path upstream beneath the modern Bolton Bridge, then passing to the side of Ferry Cottage and up onto the road beside the old Bolton Bridge. Turn left back into the village.

Embsay Crag

Distance: 3½ miles (5.5 km)
Time: 2 hours
Terrain: A mixture of field paths, moorland bridleways, grassy tracks and quiet country lanes, taking in the viewpoint of Embsay Crag (1,220 feet/371 m). The ascent up onto Embsay Crag is steep and rough underfoot.
Start: Embsay, car park near Elm Tree Square, grid ref 009538

Embsay is an attractive stone-built village on the very southern edge of the Yorkshire Dales National Park, the boundary of which runs along its main street. Rising up to the north of the village is Barden Moor, a vast swathe of heather moorland that forms a distinctive block of land between Wharfedale and Airedale. Around its edges are weathered outcrops of sandstone, the most imposing of which is Embsay Crag. Viewed from the village, its summit looks like quite a climb, but do not be deterred as its mountainous appearance is deceptive, although the final climb is quite steep. It is certainly worth the effort, as the views from the summit crags are extensive.

From the car park at the top of the village just beyond Elm Tree Square, go through the kissing-gate at the top of the car park (signposted 'Pasture Road, Eastby Road') then head to the left to reach a wall-stile in the top corner of the field. Continue across the next field, bearing slightly to the right and through a gate in a fence. Go straight on, passing the school playing fields on your left to reach another wall-stile that leads onto a farm track. Cross the track over the stile opposite, then head straight on down to reach another wall-stile in the bottom left corner of the field, after which bear slightly to the right across the field to join a corner of a fence which quickly leads to a wall-stile in the corner of the field (two houses just down to your left). Cross the wall-stile, then head straight on alongside the wall on your left and through a squeeze-stile beside a gate. Continue straight on, keeping close to the fence on your right, and down some steps onto Pasture Road opposite an old mill pond.

Turn right along the road and follow it straight on. At the junction of farm lanes, follow the road bending sharply to the right then gently rising up (ignore the turning towards Intake Farm) to reach a fork in the road at the foot of Embsay Reservoir. Take the road to the left, marked by a signpost to 'Embsay Crag', and follow this up, passing the parking area for Embsay Reservoir, just after which the road becomes a walled stony track. Follow this walled track skirting around the reservoir. Go through a gate across the track at the end of the reservoir, after which continue straight on for a short distance. Just before the track bends sharply up to the left towards Crag Nook House, turn right through a gate marked by a Barden Fell & Moor Access Information board.

There is open access across this vast moorland, which forms part of the Duke of Devonshire's Yorkshire estates, thanks to an agreement between the Yorkshire Dales National Park and the Trustees of the Chatsworth Settlement.

After the gate, head straight on along the grassy track. After a short distance the bridleway forks just as it begins to climb up. Follow the right-hand bridleway that leads down to join a wall on your right, with the reservoir just beyond the wall. Follow this wall down over a footbridge across Moor Beck. Just after this, head along the clear path bearing to the left away from the wall, climbing steadily up across the bracken-covered hillside, marked by blue waymarkers. Follow the clear path winding up towards the rocky outcrops of Embsay Crag, before a final steep climb along a rough stony path onto the summit crags.

After admiring the view, head across the top of the crags along the edge of the escarpment. Follow the clear path gradually bearing down across the hillside to the right, marked by waymarkers, to join the wall on your right. Follow this wall to reach a gate in this wall to your right just after a rectangular sheep enclosure (signposted 'Eastby'). Go through the gate, then follow the grassy path dropping down with the wall on your right to reach a gate at the top of an enclosed grassy track just after a small stream. Head through the gate and follow the wide grassy track down, with Milking Hill Wood to your right, to join a metalled lane beside Bondcroft Farm. Follow this lane straight on down to reach the road at Embsay Kirk.

Milking Hill Wood is a wonderful copse of natural woodland, untouched since at least the eighteenth century, with oak, ash, birch, rowan and hazel lining the steep slopes of the small ravine.

At the foot of this ravine stands Embsay Kirk, the original site of St Mary's and St Cuthbert's Abbey, an Augustinian priory founded around 1120 by William de Meschines, lord of Egremont, and his wife Cecily, daughter of Robert de Romille of Skipton Castle. They endowed the priory with the village of Embsay and with the churches of Skipton and Carleton. The priory moved about 1154 to Bolton Abbey, where the extensive remains can be seen today.

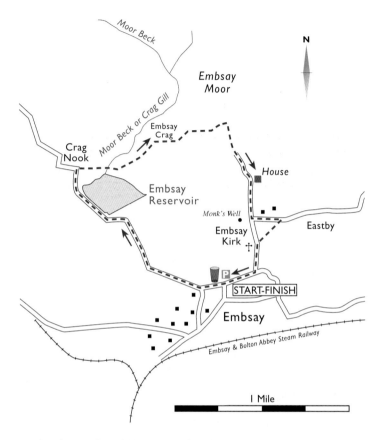

Its church at Embsay fell into ruin after the Dissolution of the Monasteries, and a large house was subsequently built on the site about 1780.

Turn left along the road and take the footpath to the right just before the first house on the right on the outskirts of Eastby. Follow the clear footpath to the right across fields to rejoin the road opposite St Mary's Church. Turn left along the road, then take the footpath to the right after a short distance through a small wall-gate. Head diagonally across the field to a stile in the opposite corner. This leads onto a short section of enclosed path, at the end of which bear left back down to the car park at Embsay.

Pinhaw

Length of Walk: 3¹/₂ miles (5.5 km)
Time: 2 hours
**Terrain: From Lothersdale, clear tracks and moorland paths lead
up to the viewpoint of Pinhaw (1,245 feet/388 m), from where
field paths and quiet lanes lead back down into the village.**
Start: Lothersdale village (on-street parking), grid ref 959459

*Lothersdale is a delightful old mill village situated in the upper reaches of
the valley of Lothersdale amongst the green folds of the South Pennines. A
large mill chimney rises up above the rooftops, a silent reminder of the
industrial heritage of this part of the Pennines, known locally as the 'heavy
woollen' district. The mill dates from 1792, and houses a forty-five-foot
waterwheel, said to be the largest internal waterwheel in the country.*

With your back to the Hare and Hounds, turn left along the main road, then
take the track up to the left between the houses (signposted 'Pennine Way')
just before you reach Lothersdale Village Hall. Follow this clear enclosed
track rising up out of the village to reach a gate across your path. After the
gate, turn left and head up the hillside, keeping close to the fence on your
left and passing a large barn just across to your right. Continue alongside
this fence, climbing steadily up then bending round to the right (the fence
becomes a stone wall). The hillside now levels out slightly. Carry straight on
alongside the wall, passing the top of the wooded stream of Stansfield Beck.
Continue climbing steadily up to reach a wall-stile beside a gate to your left
in the top corner of the field. Cross this stile, then head straight up across the
field and over another stile beside a gate that leads onto a road.

At the road, take the concrete farm lane opposite (signposted 'Pennine Way').
Follow this, rising up, then, where it bends sharp left towards Hewitts Farm,
head straight on over a wall-stile beside a gate. Walk up along the rough
grassy enclosed track, which soon opens out onto a field. Continue straight
on, keeping close to the wall on your left, to reach a wall-stile in the top left
corner of the field that leads out onto the open moorland of Carleton Moor.

Head straight on along the clear path for a short distance, then follow the
wall bending sharply round to the left. Continue alongside it. Where the wall

11

Ragged robin, water avens and spearwort all favour damp ground.

bends away to the left, carry straight on along the clear path heading up across the gently rising moorland. After a short distance, follow the path gradually bearing up to the right across the ridge of moorland to reach the trig point on Pinhaw.

What a view! Despite its modest height, this is an unbeatable vantage point with the whole of the southern Dales laid out before you, including Pendle Hill, Ingleborough, Penyghent, Buckden Pike, Simons Seat, Airedale and the Lakeland Fells on the horizon.

After admiring the view, continue straight on along the clear path dropping down the left-side of the ridge of moorland. This soon becomes a wider track, which you follow on to quickly reach a corner of a stone wall (signpost). Turn left here off the track (do not head down to the road) along a narrow path alongside the wall on your right. After a short distance (waymarker post), bear slightly to the left away from the wall along a narrow indistinct path meandering over the low 'rise' of rough heather moorland and down to reach a wall-stile near the top of a narrow plantation. Cross the wall-stile, then over another stile that leads onto an enclosed track at the top of the plantation.

Turn left along this track to quickly reach a stile beside a gate, after which head diagonally to the right down across the field to reach a wall-stile towards the far bottom corner of the field. Cross the stile, head straight down the field and over a stile that leads onto a lane beside the entrance to Calf Edge Farm. Cross the lane over the stile opposite (signposted 'Lothersdale'). Head straight down the hillside to reach a stile at the bottom of the field that leads down onto the road of White Hill Lane.

Turn right along the road to quickly reach a junction. Turn left, signed 'Lothersdale, Cross Hills', and follow the road downhill to reach the group of houses at the Fold, where you take the first turning to the right towards

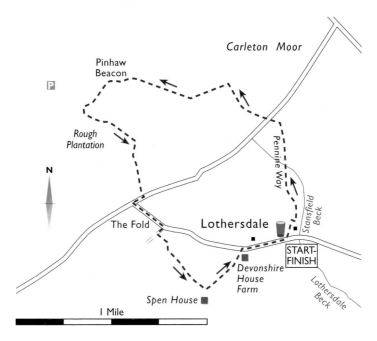

'Raygill Fisheries'. Follow this lane straight on then, after about 150 yards, turn left over a wall-stile beside a gate. Follow the track straight on (with the houses of the Fold just across to your left) to soon reach a gate that leads onto an enclosed track.

Follow this to the right over a bridge across Lothersdale Beck. After the bridge, head through the left-hand gate and follow the clear track rising up the hillside, passing above a deep wooded meander in the stream down to your left. Just after this, the track bends to the right — but we bear up to the left to join the stone wall on our left. Follow this wall, heading straight up the hillside to reach a wall-stile to your left in the top left corner of the field just below Spen House Farm.

Cross the stile and head straight on alongside the small stream on your right, through an old metal kissing-gate (ignore the grass-covered bridge). Go down alongside the stream on your right to reach a gate that leads into the yard of Devonshire House Farm (marked as Lower Spen House on the OS map). Head straight on through the yard and follow the lane down to reach the road opposite the old mill pond, where you turn right along the road back into Lothersdale.

13

Bolton Priory

Length of walk: 4½ miles (7 km)
Time: 2½ hours
Terrain: Clear riverside and woodland footpaths, including some permissive paths, through the beautiful Bolton Abbey Estate
Start: Cavendish Pavilion, Bolton Abbey (small fee payable), grid ref 078551

Bolton Abbey is perhaps Wharfedale's most famous landmark. Strictly speaking, though, this name relates only to the village adjacent to the ruins of Bolton Priory, established in 1154 by a group of Augustinian canons. There is much to explore here, with the foundations of the monastic priory buildings clearly visible to the south of the church.

From the Cavendish Pavilion, head back along the driveway towards the parking area and over a cattle grid. Bear left along the riverside road, with the River Wharfe on your left, that leads through the parking area. At the end of the driveway and parking area, a gravel path leads on to quickly reach a kissing-gate. Follow the clear path across a field, then up some steps onto the road beside the Cavendish Memorial Fountain.

This memorial was built to commemorate Lord Frederick, Chief Secretary to Ireland and son of the seventh duke of Devonshire, who was assassinated in Phoenix Park, Dublin, in 1882.

Turn left along the roadside footpath, then head through a gate that leads into the churchyard of Bolton Priory (Church of St Mary and St Cuthbert), marked by a signpost 'Barden Bridge, Bolton Bridge, Storiths'. Walk straight on, passing the main west door, then head to the left across the priory ruins down to join a clear riverside path beside a footbridge and stepping stones. Do not cross the footbridge, but turn right along this path. Almost immediately, bear off to the left along a grassy riverside path that leads to a riverbank stile. Follow the riverside path straight on across fields to eventually reach the road just to the right of Bolton Bridge across the Wharfe.

Turn left over Bolton Bridge, then take the enclosed footpath to the left, marked by a signpost 'footpath to Priory Footbridge' just before Red Lion

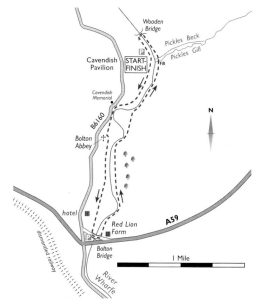

Farm. The enclosed path soon leads to a stile, after which head straight on across the field to quickly join the river (and fence) on your left. Follow the clear path gently rising up a small bank, still with the fence and river on your left, to reach a stile above the steep riverbank. Head over the stile and carry straight on along the top of the bank to quickly join a rough track, which you follow down to river level.

A clear path now leads on across flat pastures through gates heading towards Bolton Priory in the distance. At the end of these pastures, you cross a small footbridge over a side-stream and then a stile. Follow the footpath up the bank ahead, keeping close to the fence on your left, to run along the top of a steep wooded bank that leads to a stile beside a gate. After the gate, head left alongside the fence on your left, then turn left along an enclosed footpath to quickly reach a stile, with superb views of Bolton Priory through the trees ahead. Cross the stile and follow the clear stony path to the right along the top of the bank, to quickly reach a junction of paths (signposted 'Bolton Priory'). Here, head left down to reach a junction with another path.

At this junction, take the grassy path down to the right that heads across pastures to join a clear riverside path that leads to a stile. Follow the clear stony path through the woods, with the River Wharfe on your left. Climb up through the woods to join another path coming in from your right. Follow this clear undulating path to the left, meandering high above the river through the woods, to eventually join a road. Turn left along the road, down over a ford/footbridge across Pickles Beck, then turn left (signposted 'Cavendish Pavilion') along a footpath that leads down over a stile beside a gate. Follow the clear riverside path to reach the wooden bridge, where you turn left over the bridge back to the Cavendish Pavilion.

15

Jubilee Tower

Length of walk: 4¹/₂ miles (7 km)
Time: 2¹/₂ hours
Terrain: Canal towpaths, old tracks, field paths and heather moorland. This walk involves numerous squeeze-stiles, wall-stiles and ladder-stiles, whilst the climb up onto Farnhill Moor to reach the Jubilee Tower is steep.
Start: Kildwick (on-street parking), grid ref 012458

Kildwick lies in the heart of Airedale, its quiet streets a pleasure to explore as there is much of interest to see, including a medieval bridge and the superb Jacobean Kildwick Hall. Dominating the village is St Andrew's Church, which is known locally as the 'Long Church of Craven' due to its unusually large nave. Britain's longest inland waterway, the Leeds-Liverpool Canal, passes through the heart of the village. The canal took forty-six years to complete and was opened fully in 1816.

From the steps up to St Andrew's Church beside the war memorial in the centre of Kildwick, head up along Priest Bank Road to reach Barrett's Bridge (swing bridge) across the Leeds-Liverpool Canal. Turn right before this bridge along the canal towpath. Follow this clear canalside path for half a mile to reach another swing bridge (Grange Bridge). Turn left across this bridge and over a stile beside a gate. Head up the hillside alongside the fence/wall on your right, which soon becomes a grassy track that leads up to reach the road opposite the houses of Kildwick Grange.

Turn left along the road then, after about 100 yards, turn right along the lane towards 'Kildwick Grange'. Follow this lane up then, where it forks just after Grange Farm, follow the right-hand lane up, passing some houses on your right, to reach a gate across your path just beyond Hainsworth House Farm (at the end of the stony lane). Head through the gate and follow the track rising up through woodland, which soon becomes a rough grassy track enclosed by walls. Continue up along this enclosed track for a further 100 yards, then turn left through a squeeze-stile. Head straight on over a wall-stile just ahead. After the stile, head up alongside the wall on your left for a short distance then, where this wall bends slightly to the right, cross the wall-stile to the left. Bear to the right across the field and over a stile in a

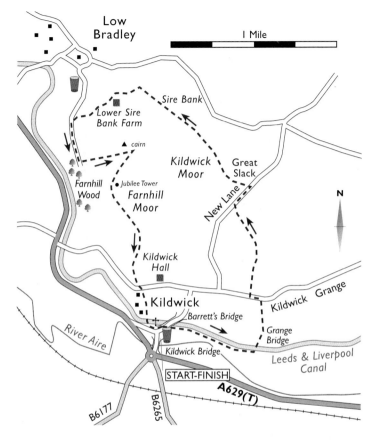

small section of wall. Bear right over another wall-stile, then straight on through a gate, just to the right of the barn, which leads onto New Lane.

Turn right along the road, passing Great Slack Farm on your right. Just after, turn left through a gate and follow the rough track up alongside the wall on your right to reach a ladder-stile beside a gate at the top of the field. Cross the ladder-stile and continue up alongside the wall, passing a small copse of woodland, to reach another ladder-stile beside a gate just beyond the woodland. Cross the stile, then bear to the left across the field through a squeeze-stile at the top of the field. Head left to join the wall on your left, which you follow to another squeeze-stile in the field corner (beside another copse of woodland).

After this stile, head straight on alongside the wall on your left and over a wall-stile. Continue on across the next field, still with the wall on your left, to reach another wall-stile to your left in the field corner. Cross the stile and turn right to quickly reach another wall-stile. Head straight on alongside the wall on your right, dropping down (with Sirebank House just across to your left) over two wall-stiles, then on through a bridle-gate that leads onto a farm lane. Turn right down this lane, then over a wall-stile to the left of the cattle grid at the bottom of the field, and onto a metalled lane.

Turn left along the lane for a short distance. Where the wall ends on your right, cross the wall-stile to the right that leads out onto a field. Head to the right, down across the field, to a wall-stile in the bottom corner. Over the stile, continue straight on alongside the wall on your right, passing below Lower Sirebank Farm, over two wall-stiles and then out onto a larger field. Follow the grassy track straight on, towards the house ahead, passing above two concealed storage tanks, then slant down very gently across the hillside through a large gap in the wall just to the right of the house. Continue straight on over a stile that leads onto the road opposite Hamblethorpe Farm.

Turn left along the road for a quarter of a mile to reach Wood Cottage in Farnhill Wood. At the cottage, turn left off the road up alongside the wall on your left, climbing steeply up through the woods. Clamber up some low sandstone outcrops, still with the wall on your left. The hillside levels out slightly, before climbing up another bank onto the heather moorland of Farnhill Moor. Carry straight on up across the gently rising moorland (alongside the wall) to reach a bench at the top of the hill. At the bench, turn right back on yourself slightly, along a clear path across the heather moorland to reach Jubilee Tower.

The tower, built in 1935 to commemorate the silver jubilee of King George V, has extensive views across Airedale from Skipton down towards Keighley.

From the tower, follow the clear path straight on, gently dropping down for a short distance. Where the path divides, follow the left-hand path, gradually dropping down across the heather moorland for half a mile, to reach a gate in a wall just to the right of Crag Top Farm. Head through the gate and follow the path straight on, passing above some old quarry workings. Where the path divides as you approach some woodland, head straight on down through the woods, passing to the side of a house, to join the road at Farnhill. Turn left along the road then, after a short distance, turn right along Starkey Lane. Follow this down to reach the canal across your path at the bottom of the hill. Turn left and cross the bridge over the canal, then follow the path down alongside the churchyard back into Kildwick.

Skipton Moor

Length of walk: 5 miles (8 km)
Time: 2¹/₂ hours
Terrain: High-level tracks and moorland paths all the way. Some
sections of this walk follow indistinct paths across boggy
moorland — route-finding may be difficult in poor weather.
Start: The top of Shortbank Road, Skipton, grid ref 002512.
Alternative start: **Skipton Market Place (adds 1³/₄ miles/3 km to the**
walk). From the bottom of the market place, head along
Newmarket Street and follow this straight on for just under a mile
(it joins Shortbank Road) all the way up to the top of the road.

*Skipton has been an important town for many centuries, as it guards one of
the few low-level routes across the Pennines, known as the Aire Gap. Robert
de Romille, a Norman baron, built a castle on the crags above Eller Beck. In
1310 Edward II granted the castle to Robert Clifford, who became the first
Lord Clifford of Skipton and subsequently rebuilt the castle as a stone fortress.*

From the top of Shortbank Road, head straight up along the rough enclosed track. Where this opens out into an area of woodland, follow the path bending up to the right alongside the wall and through an area of gorse bushes. The path bends to the left away from the wall to quickly emerge on level ground, with an old quarry to your right and the steep wooded bank to your left.

Head straight on along the top of this wooded bank along a clear wide path, which gently

The gateway of Skipton Castle.

19

rises and quickly opens out onto a wide track with views to your left. Continue straight on along this track, which heads up through an area of deciduous woodland, after which the track levels out. Carry straight on along this high-level enclosed grassy track for a further mile until you reach a bridle-gate in a wall across your path just beside a plantation on your left. Do not head through this bridle-gate, but cross the wall-stile just to your right that leads out onto the grassy moorland of Skipton Moor.

Turn left alongside the wall and follow the narrow path straight on, running parallel with the track on your left, to cross an area of boggy ground. Soon after, turn sharp right away from the wall (waymarker). Follow the narrow path straight on across the moorland, over an area of boggy ground after about 100 yards. Then follow the path to the left (waymarker) slanting gradually up across the moorland, to reach a gate in a fence corner at the top of the moor. Head through the gate and follow the track straight on then bending round to the left. Just after it bends to the right towards Snow Hill Farm, cross the stile beside the gate to your left. Head to the right down across the field to reach a gate immediately to the right of a plantation. Head through the gate and walk along the concrete track to quickly reach another gate. This leads onto a 'junction' of concrete farm lanes just to the left of the buildings of Snow Hill Farm.

At this junction, head through the gate opposite. Bear to the right across the paddock and over a stile in the opposite corner. Turn left through a gate onto a farm lane. Head through the metal gate opposite, then turn right alongside the fence on your right, passing in front of the farmhouse. Where this fence bears away to the right, continue straight on down to reach a wall-stile at the bottom of the field. Cross the stile, then head straight down through a gate in a wall at the bottom of the field, just to the right of Middleborough House.

Continue on to quickly reach a rutted track across your path just after the farm buildings. Turn right along this track and through the left-hand of two gates at the other side of the field. After the gate, turn right alongside the wall and head up through two gates. Carry straight on, bearing very slightly away from the wall, to reach a gate in a fence where it joins a wall. After the gate, continue straight on alongside the wall on your left to reach a wall-stile to your left just before High Edge Farm.

Cross the stile, then turn right over another wall-stile that leads onto the lane just below High Edge. Head straight on over the low wall ahead, then across the front garden of High Edge and through a wall gap. Pass to the left of the greenhouse and through another gap. After this, turn left over a wall-stile just above Low Edge Farm. Go down over a small bridge across a stream and up over a stile. Walk up the small bank and head to the right, keeping

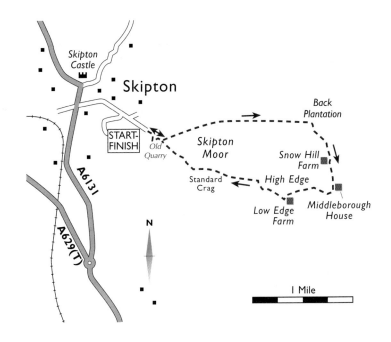

close to the gorse bushes on your right at first, then bear left across the rough grassy hillside (no clear path) to reach a gate in the tumbledown wall halfway up the hillside on the other side of the field. After the gate, turn right up across the moorland to reach a wall-stile at the top of the field. Cross the stile, then turn left alongside the wall and follow this for three-quarters of a mile to reach the outcrops of Standard Crag.

Follow the path straight on across the top of the outcrops to reach a clear sunken path just after the outcrops by a wall-stile on your left. Turn right down along the path, with a wall just across to your left, and follow this, winding down across the rough hillside to reach a wall-stile across your path just to the left of a gate. Head over this wall-stile and follow the grassy track straight on for about 200 yards. Where the track forks, follow the right-hand path, dropping down to reach a stile hidden amongst gorse bushes at the bottom of the field, and onto the track near the old quarry. Turn left along the track and retrace your steps back down through the woodland, then along the enclosed track to reach the top of Shortbank Road.

Cononley Ings

Length of walk: 5 miles (8 km)
Time: 2¹/₂ hours
Terrain: A riverside path leads alongside the Aire all the way to the hamlet of Cononley Woodside, from where there is a fairly steep climb up onto the heather moorland of Burnt Hill. Field paths then lead steadily back down into Cononley.
Start: Cononley (on-street parking), grid ref 990469

Cononley is a delightful old village that lies sheltered in the small side-valley of Cononley Beck. First settled by Saxon farmers over a millennium ago, Cononley remained a small agricultural village until the the onset of the Industrial Revolution, when the leadmines on the hills behind the village were expanded, large textile mills were built between the village and the River Aire, and rows of workers' cottages sprang up.

From the centre of Cononley, walk down along Main Street through the village, over the level crossing across the railway line. Continue along the road out of the village, passing the large mill on your left, to soon reach the bridge across the River Aire. Turn left before this bridge (signpost) down some steps onto the riverside path. Head straight on along the riverside path, with the River Aire on your right, over a stile then on through a kissing-gate. Carry straight on along the riverside path alongside a large grass-covered levée on your left for three-quarters of a mile through a series of kissing-gates, until you reach a track enclosed by hedges just across to your left.

Do not head onto this track, but continue straight on along the riverside path (with the track just across to your left) for a quarter of a mile until the path joins this track. Head straight on along the track for a short distance, then bear off to the right along the riverside path, leaving the track to cross over the levée. Follow this riverside path to soon reach a concrete outfall and a fence across your path. Turn left over the levée, then bear slightly to the left across the field, heading towards the bridge across the railway, to reach a gate in a fence and a bridge across the side-stream of Dead Eye, and onto an enclosed track. Follow this track up to reach the railway bridge. Turn right immediately after the bridge through a kissing-gate, then head to the left up across the field over two stiles and onto a track.

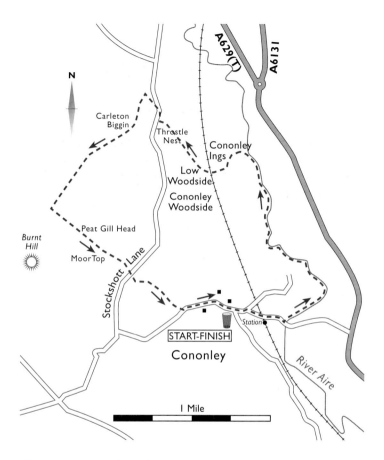

Head straight on along the track, passing above the houses of Low Woodside. Follow this track down over a cattle grid and on towards a house. As you approach the house, branch off the track skirting to the right of the house and garden, over a small stream and alongside the hedge to reach a gate just beyond the house. Head through the gate. Follow the enclosed track bending to the left behind the house then round to the right. At this point, cross the stile to the right over the fence.

Turn left alongside the fence (and track) and pass to the right side of Throstle Nest House to reach a gate tucked away in the corner of a wall just beyond the house. Head through the gate and go straight on along the grassy

23

track up across the field to reach another gate, after which follow the grassy track straight on for a short distance. Head off the track to the right, slanting up across the hillside to reach a bridlegate at the top of the field that leads onto the road (signpost).

At the road, take the footpath opposite to the right up some steps, then immediately over another stile that leads out onto a field. Head to the right across the field to reach a ladder-stile that leads onto a lane. Turn left up to reach the entrance gates to Carleton Biggin House, just before which follow the enclosed path to the right that quickly leads to a wall-stile to the right of the entrance gates. Cross the stile and head alongside the wall on your left up through a gate in the top corner of the field. Head straight on, climbing steeply up the ridge of land alongside the wall on your left, to reach a wall-stile across your path that leads out onto heather moorland. Carry straight on up alongside the wall on your left onto the top of the moor. Continue on across the crest of the hill to reach a wall across your path and a gate just to your left in a small 'dip' in the moorland.

Head left through the gate and walk straight on (no clear path) across the rough moorland, heading towards Peat Gill Head Farm ahead. Skirt to the left of the boggy ground at the foot of the small bank, to join a small section of wall on your left that quickly leads to a wall-stile across your path (at the top of a line of mature trees). Cross the stile and head through the wall gap ahead. Walk straight on alongside the wall on your left down to reach a squeeze-stile in the bottom corner of the field, which leads onto a track (Peat Gill Head Farm to your left). Head straight on along the track, passing in front of the farmhouse, then, where this track bends to the left, go straight on across the field to reach a wall-stile across your path. Cross the stile and head across the field, bearing to the left up to a wall-stile in the top left corner in front of Moor Top House, that leads onto a lane. Turn right along the lane and follow it down to reach the road.

At the road, take the footpath opposite over a wall-stile (signpost) and head straight down across the field over another wall-stile. After this stile, turn left alongside the wall on your left around the top edge of the field, then down to a squeeze-stile in the bottom left corner of the field. Cross the stile and head straight on down the hillside alongside a small wooded stream, to reach a gate to the left of a house. This leads onto the road, where you turn left down into Cononley.

Flasby Fell

Length of walk: 6 miles (9.5 km)
Time: 3 hours
Terrain: Moorland paths and forest tracks with a short section
along a quiet country lane. The initial climb out of Flasby up onto
Flasby Fell is quite steep, reaching a height of 1,030 feet (315 m).
Start: Flasby village (limited on-street parking), grid ref 947566

*The scattered hamlet of Flasby lies hidden away amongst the rolling hills of
Airedale. A handful of old stone cottages and farms line the narrow lane that
leads down to a bridge across Flasby Beck.*

From the centre of Flasby, follow the lane down passing Grange Farm,
marked by a 'Dead End' sign, over the bridge across Flasby Beck and up to
reach the next farmhouse, where the lane divides. Follow the track straight
on (ignore the track to the right towards Stirton), passing in front of the
farmhouse. Where the track forks again, head straight on through the gate
(signposted 'Grassington Road'). Follow the enclosed track, which rises up
through woodland and then levels out, leaving the woodland behind.
Continue straight on to reach a gate across the path at the end of the enclosed
track. Head through the gate and bear to the left up across the field to reach
a metal gate halfway up the field in the wall opposite.

Head through the gate and follow the grassy path straight on, climbing up
across Flasby Fell, heading towards the 'twin' outcrops above, with a small
wooded stream just down to your right. The path bears gently up to the left
and crosses the top of the small stream, then heads steadily upwards (boggy
in places), keeping close to the wall on your left. Continue heading up across
the moor then, where the wall turns sharply away to the left as you approach
the foot of the outcrops of Rough Haw, follow the path bearing to the right
across the hillside, passing to the right-hand side of the outcrops to join a
clearer path (waymarked). Follow this to the left, soon reaching a bridle-gate
in a wall at the top of Flasby Fell.

*Flasby Fell, rising up to the east of the hamlet of the same name, is a large
wedge of moorland sandwiched between Skipton, Gargrave and Hetton.
Standing proud above this moorland are the gritstone peaks of Sharp Haw*

and Rough Haw. These prominent landmarks dominate the skyline and, once climbed, are instantly recognisable, and will have you glancing back in admiration every time you drive through Skipton. Sharp Haw, as its name suggests, is a narrow outcrop of rock that rises up like the crest of a huge wave.

Go straight through the bridle-gate, then head straight on along the clear but boggy path winding up for about 200 yards. Where the path forks just by an isolated hawthorn tree, follow the path bending sharply round to the left (ignore a path straight on up towards the Trig Point on Sharp Haw), to soon reach a gate in a wall. Go through the gate and head straight on along the clear wide path, across the open grassy moorland. Follow this path straight on, gradually dropping down for three-quarters of a mile to reach a gate in a wire fence across your route (with Skyrakes Farm some distance across to your left). Head through the gate and continue along the wide grassy path, dropping down then bearing very slightly to the right to join a clear stony track, which you follow straight on over cattle grids to join the road.

Turn right along the road and follow it around four sharp bends before dropping gently down, passing Tarn House Farm. Just after the farm, take the footpath to the right over a wall-stile (signposted 'Flasby'). Head straight on across the field and over a wall-stile beside a gate in the bottom left corner. Carry straight on, keeping close to the fence on your left. Follow it, bending up to the right, then cross a stile over this fence to the left.Turn right (with the fence now on your right) and follow the clear grassy path up to reach a wall-stile beside a gate at the top of the field. Cross the stile, then go alongside the wall on your right to reach a stile and gate in the top corner of the field. Cross the stile and walk along the raised grassy path across rough moorland and down over a small wooded stream. Continue straight on to reach a wall-stile that leads into a plantation, about fifty yards to the left from the gate in the wall. (Please note: forestry operations are ongoing and the appearance of this plantation may change; please observe forestry warning notices.)

Cross the stile and follow the path along the edge of the plantation (recently felled area to your right) and out into a clearing. Continue on, bearing gradually up to the right, to quickly join the clear forestry track. Turn left along this clear track and follow it, gently rising up. Then, where the track divides after a short distance, follow the right-hand track rising up across the hillside, with gritstone outcrops above. Continue straight on along this track, which soon levels out and leads on through the forest of Crag Wood (recent felling has opened up views towards Gargrave) for a further three-quarters of a mile (1 km), before dropping quite steeply down then bending very sharply round to the left. Here, take the footpath straight on (to the right) off

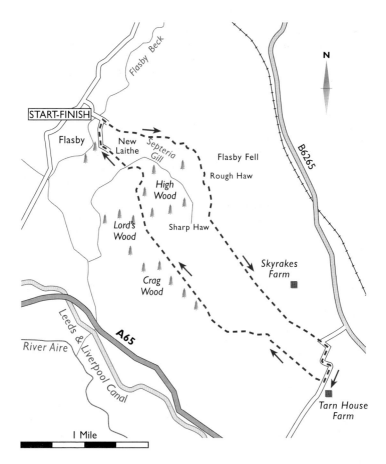

this bend, marked by a signpost 'Flasby'. Follow the clear narrow path through rhododendrons to soon join a clearer path. Follow this straight on, steadily dropping down and gradually curving to the right, to reach a gate at the end of the woods.

Head through the gate and follow the clear grassy track across the field, curving down to the left to reach a gate that leads onto an enclosed track and a bridge across Septeria Gill. Cross the bridge and follow the track straight on, passing a cottage and then some large barns. Continue along the track, which drops down and then bends to the right back down into Flasby. As you enter the hamlet, follow the lane to the left over the bridge into its centre.

Haw Crag

Length of walk: 6 miles (9.5 km)
Time: 3 hours
**Terrain: Field paths initially, then quiet country lanes and a
muddy track. After a short section of road walking, a farm lane
then field paths lead up to Haw Crag, from where there are
superb views. The old enclosed track of Mark House Lane leads
all the way back to Gargrave.**
Start: Gargrave (car parks on West and North Streets), grid ref 933543

*The old coaching village of Gargrave lies in the heart of Airedale, where
road, river, canal and railway compete for space along the valley floor.
Gargrave is surrounded by low, undulating hills known as drumlins, created
by retreating glaciers many thousands of years ago, which, combined with
the close proximity of the meandering rivers Aire and Ribble, have made this
one of the few low-level routes across the Pennines, known as the Aire Gap.
The Pennine Way also heads through the village on its 268-mile (430 km)
trek from Edale in the Peak District to Kirk Yetholm in Scotland, Gargrave
marking the start of its journey through the Yorkshire Dales.*

From the centre of Gargrave, walk along the main A65 road towards
Skipton. Just before you leave the village, turn left along Eshton Road. Go
along this road heading out of the village, over a bridge across the Leeds-
Liverpool Canal, and bending round to the right. Continue straight on along
the road. Where the houses end on your right just after the 'Gargrave
village' road-sign, take the path to the left over a wall-stile beside a gate
(signposted 'Eshton').

*You are about to walk through the former parkland of Eshton Hall, a fine
early nineteenth-century house that was once the home of the Wilson family,
who acquired the estate back in the seventeenth century. The hall has
recently been redeveloped into luxury homes.*

Cross the stile, then head to the right across the field, bearing away from the
road (following a line of mature trees) to reach a metal stile over a fence.
Cross this and head left up across the hillside to reach a kissing-gate in a
fence that leads into Gamsbers Wood. Follow the clear path through the

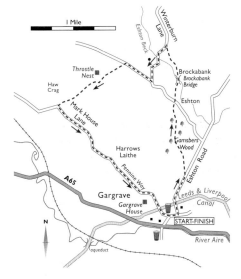

woods, passing a house set in a clearing, to a kissing-gate at the end of the woods. Go through the gate, bear left across the field and over a stile across a fence. Continue straight on to reach another stile in the far right corner of the field, after which turn right over a wall-stile onto the road.

Cross the stile opposite to the left, signposted 'Winterburn Lane'. Head straight across the field to a stile in the bottom left corner. Cross this and continue on along the top of the steep grassy bank, with Eshton Beck down to your right, gently curving down to reach a stile beside a gate that leads onto a lane. Turn right along the lane and follow it down over Brockabank Bridge, then up to reach Brockabank Farm.

As you reach the farm gates, head left along the grassy bridleway passing in front of the farmhouse, with the steep wooded banks of Eshton Beck to your left, to reach a gate across your path just beyond the house. Through the gate, head straight on alongside the wall and wooded riverbank on your left. Where this wall bends away, continue straight on to quickly join another wall on your left at the start of a clear track, which you follow straight on to join the road (Winterburn Lane).

A short detour along the road to the right brings you to Friars Head farmhouse, a magnificent seventeenth-century yeoman's farmhouse with four well-proportioned bays and lots of mullion windows. This house is said to stand on the site of a monastic farm that once belonged to Furness Abbey.

Turn left along the road and follow this down over a bridge across Eshton Beck. Continue up, passing St Helens Well on your right, and along the road to reach a T-junction with the Malham road. Turn right along the road towards 'Airton, Malham' (take extra care on this stretch, walking in single file and facing oncoming traffic). Follow this uphill for just less than half a

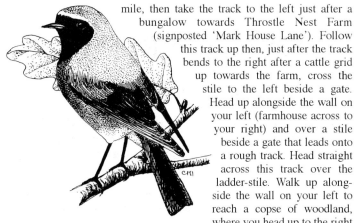

mile, then take the track to the left just after a bungalow towards Throstle Nest Farm (signposted 'Mark House Lane'). Follow this track up then, just after the track bends to the right after a cattle grid up towards the farm, cross the stile to the left beside a gate. Head up alongside the wall on your left (farmhouse across to your right) and over a stile beside a gate that leads onto a rough track. Head straight across this track over the ladder-stile. Walk up alongside the wall on your left to reach a copse of woodland, where you head up to the right alongside the fence/woodland, to cross a stile beside a bridle-gate at the top of the field.

The redstart is an attractively coloured bird which inhabits open woodland.

Walk straight on up across the open field. As the field levels out, bear slightly to the right to reach a wall-stile beside a gate at the top of the field, with the trig point on Haw Crag just ahead. Head through the gate then walk straight on, keeping close to the fence on your left, passing some old quarry workings on your right below Haw Crag, to join a rough track. Follow this down through a gate at the bottom of the field that leads onto a junction of tracks.

Despite its modest height, Haw Crag affords wonderful views, with Pendle Hill, the rugged skyline of Flasby Fell, Rylstone Fell, the Winterburn Valley and the upper reaches of Airedale clearly visible.

Turn left along the walled track (Mark House Lane). Follow this, gently rising up then levelling out, before dropping steadily down (the track becoming a rougher stony bridleway for a while) to reach the large stone barn of Harrows Laithe on your left after about a mile. Continue straight on along the enclosed track, which becomes much clearer and soon becomes a metalled lane. Follow this all the way back down into Gargrave. As you reach the outskirts of Gargrave, the lane skirts around the walled gardens of Gargrave House to reach a road junction, where you head straight on over a bridge across the canal into Gargrave.

Winterburn Reservoir

> **Length of Walk: 6 miles (9.5 km)**
> **Time: 3 hours**
> **Terrain: Clear enclosed tracks, field paths alongside Winterburn**
> **Reservoir and then a quiet country lane to finish.**
> **Start: Hetton (on-street parking), grid ref 962588**

The small village of Hetton lies off the beaten track between Skipton and Grassington. Its long single street is lined with old stone houses, at the heart of which is the Angel Inn, formerly an old droving pub in the eighteenth century.

With your back to the Angel Inn, turn left along the road. Just before you leave the village, turn left along a track beside a small triangular green enclosed by railings that leads up through a gate (signposted 'Hetton Common'). Follow the stony enclosed track (Moor Lane), rising steadily up the hillside. Pass a track off to the left after three-quarters of a mile, and continue to the top of the rise. The track levels out and leads on (now a grassy enclosed track) for a further three-quarters of a mile (1 km) to reach a gate across your path at the end of the walled track, marked by a five-finger signpost.

Head through the gate and follow the slightly raised gravel path straight on (signposted 'Malham'), slanting very gradually to the left down across the hillside, to reach a bridge across Hetton Common Beck at the head of Winterburn Reservoir. Cross the bridge, then turn left (signposted 'Winterburn') with the stream on your left, over a small side-stream. Just beyond this is a ladder-stile and gate beside the head of the reservoir. Cross the ladder-stile, then walk straight on alongside the wall and reservoir on your left to reach a wall-stile across your path. Over the wall-stile, continue straight on, still with the reservoir on your left, to reach a small footbridge across the side-stream of Park Gill. After the footbridge (and two bridle-gates), carry straight on alongside the fence and reservoir. Where you reach a small inlet and side-stream across your path, follow the fence-line bending up to the right along the top of a small but steep bank above this side-stream (heading away from the reservoir), to reach a wall-stile that leads onto a clear farm lane.

Winterburn Reservoir, hidden away amongst the hills, was built during the 1890s as a supply reservoir for the Leeds-Liverpool Canal.

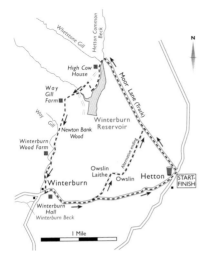

Turn left along the lane and go down over a bridge across Way Gill, after which follow the lane bending up to the left then, after a short distance, take the path to the right over a stile beside a gate (signpost). Head straight up across the field to reach a gate on your left, just to the left side of Way Gill Farm at the top of the field (signpost). Head through the gate and walk alongside the fence on your right to reach the farm lane just beside the entrance to the farm. Turn left along this lane and follow it straight on and then bending sharply round to the left.

Soon after, turn right off the track over a stone wall-stile beside a gate. Head down the field, keeping close to the fence and grassy ditch on your left, to reach a wall-stile beside a gate at the bottom of the field. Cross the stile, then continue straight on down across the field, keeping fairly close to the wall/plantation on your right to reach a stile in a fence across your path just beside the edge of the plantation (at the top of a steep bank above the Winterburn Valley). Cross the stile, then bear slightly to the left down the hillside to reach a gate that leads onto a lane.

Turn right along the lane and follow this down, passing Winterburn Wood Farm. The lane bends to the left over a bridge across Winterburn Beck, then curves round to the right, heading down alongside the stream to reach the hamlet of Winterburn. Head straight on along the road through the hamlet to reach a T-junction. At the T-junction, turn left towards 'Hetton, Grassington' and follow this quiet country lane for one and three-quarter miles back to Hetton.

Alternative ending (adds extra ³/₄ mile): At the T-junction, turn left and follow the road. Where it levels out, head left through a gate (signposted 'Moor Lane'). Follow the grassy track straight on, keeping close to the wall on your right, passing two barns then follow the wall bending sharp right to reach a gate in the wall corner. Head straight on along the enclosed track, bending round to the left at Owslin Farm (now a barn) and through a gate. Continue up along the track (Cross Lane) to reach Moor Lane, which you follow to the right into Hetton.

32